THE
POWER
OF CHOICE

A Teen's Guide to Making Good

Decisions

ANTONIO R. BROADNAX M. ED

THE
POWER
OF CHOICE

A Teen's Guide to Making

Good Decisions

Contents

INTRODUCTION

Definition of choice and its importance

The concept of choice is one of the most important aspects of human life. It refers to the ability to make decisions and select one option from among several alternatives. Every day, we make choices that shape our lives, and the decisions we make can have a significant impact on our future.

Choice is an integral part of personal development and growth. It allows us to take control of our lives and make decisions that align with our goals and values. When we make choices, we exercise our autonomy, and this is crucial in building self-esteem and confidence.

The importance of choice cannot be overstated. It is through the choices we make that we create our destiny. Every choice we make has consequences, and we must be conscious of the impact of our decisions. By understanding the power of choice, we can make more informed decisions that lead to a fulfilling life.

Teens, in particular, need to understand the importance of choice. They are at a stage where they explore their identity and make decisions that will shape their future. They need to know that they have the power to choose and that their choices can have an impact on their lives.

Parents also play a crucial role in teaching their children about the power of choice. By giving them the freedom to make decisions and experience the consequences of their choices, parents can help their children develop critical thinking skills and decision-making abilities.

Life coaching, personal development coaching, and leadership coaching are all geared towards helping individuals take control of their lives and make informed decisions. These coaches help individuals identify their goals and values, and then work with them to develop a plan of action that aligns with those goals and values.

Hey let me tell you something exciting! The concept of choice is essential for your personal growth and development. You get to create your own destiny through choices, and that is super empowering! It's all about understanding the power of choice and making informed decisions that will help you live your best life. And guess what? By teaching teens and kids about the importance of choice and working with coaches to develop critical thinking skills, we can help them take charge of their lives and reach their goals. How cool is that? Let's go make some awesome choices!

How choices affect everything in life

The choices we make in life have a significant impact on who we are and who we become. From the food we eat to the career we pursue, every decision we make influences our present and future. It is important for teens, parents, and coaches to understand how choices affect everything in life.

As a teen, the choices you make can shape your future. Your academic and career choices can determine the path you take in life. Your social and personal choices can affect your mental health and overall well-being. One bad decision can lead to a lifetime of regret, while a good one can open doors to endless possibilities.

As a parent, you play a crucial role in guiding your children towards making good choices. It is important to foster an environment of open communication where your children feel comfortable discussing their thoughts and concerns. Encourage them to think critically and weigh the pros and cons of every decision they make. Teach them to take responsibility for their choices and the consequences that come with them.

As a life coach, personal development coach, or leadership coach, your role is to help individuals make informed decisions that align with their goals and values. By empowering them to take charge of their lives, you can help them become more resilient, confident, and successful. Encourage them to identify their strengths and weaknesses and work towards self-improvement.

In conclusion, the power of choice is a vital aspect of our lives. Every decision we make has consequences that can impact our present and future. As teens, parents, and coaches, we must understand how choices affect everything in life and work towards making informed decisions that reflect our values and goals. By doing so, we can create a life of purpose, fulfillment, and happiness.

The purpose of the book

The purpose of this book, "The Power of Choice: A Teen's Guide to Making Good Decisions," is to provide teenagers with the tools they need to make informed decisions that will positively impact their lives. As teenagers navigate the challenges of adolescence, they are faced with countless choices that can have lasting effects on their future.

This book aims to empower teens to take control of their lives by teaching them how to make decisions that align with their values and goals. By learning to make informed choices, teens can avoid the pitfalls that often accompany impulsive decision-making.

Parents can also benefit from reading this book, as it provides them with valuable insights into the decision-making process of their teenagers. By understanding the thought processes behind their teen's choices, parents can better support them and guide them towards making responsible decisions.

The niches of Life Coaching, Personal Development Coaching, and Leadership Coaching can also benefit from this book. Coaches can use the principles outlined in this book to help their clients develop effective decision-making skills, which are essential for success in all areas of life.

Overall, the purpose of this book is to provide teenagers with a roadmap for making good decisions that will set them up for success in the future. By empowering teens to take control of their lives and make informed choices, we can help them build a bright and prosperous future for themselves.

UNDERSTANDING CHOICES

The different types of choices

The Different Types of Choices

Did you know that in life, we make choices all the time? Some of them are small, like picking what to wear or eat, but others are way more significant, like choosing a career or where to go to college. Knowing the different types of choices can help you make better decisions and take control of your life. Check it out:

1. Habitual Choices: These are the ones we make automatically, like brushing our teeth or checking our phone. By making positive habitual choices, we can create healthy habits that lead to a happier and more fulfilling life.

2. Emotional Choices: These are based on our feelings and can be influenced by our mood or stress levels. They can be impulsive and not always the best decision. It's essential to be aware of your emotions and how they may affect your choices.

3. Rational Choices: These are based on logic and reason, and they're usually well thought out and based on facts and information. They're crucial for significant decisions like choosing a college major or buying a car.

4. Intuitive Choices: These are based on our gut feelings, and they can be helpful when making tough decisions or facing a difficult situation. Trusting your intuition can lead to positive outcomes. Knowing the different types of choices can help you make better decisions and create a happier life. So remember, the power of choice is in your hands!

The power of choice and its impact on one's life

The Power of Choice and Its Impact on One's Life

We all have the power to make choices in our lives, whether big or small. These choices can have a significant impact on our future and the direction our lives take. The power of choice is a fundamental concept that every teenager, parent, and individual seeking personal development, leadership coaching, or life coaching should understand.

The choices we make can determine our success, happiness, and well-being. It is important to make good choices that align with our values, goals, and aspirations. Good choices lead to positive outcomes, while poor choices can have negative consequences that can affect our lives for years to come.

The power of choice is a gift that we must use wisely. As teenagers, you have a lot of choices to make, from what subjects to study, what extracurricular activities to participate in, and who to hang out with. These choices may seem insignificant, but they can shape your future. It is essential to make choices that will help you achieve your goals and lead a fulfilling life.

As parents, you play a crucial role in helping your teenagers make good choices. You can provide guidance, support, and advice to help them make informed decisions. Encourage them to think critically, weigh their options, and consider the consequences of their choices.

For life coaches, personal development coaches, and leadership coaches, the power of choice is a fundamental concept that underpins your coaching philosophy. As a coach, you help individuals identify their values, goals, and aspirations and empower them to make choices that align with these principles. You help individuals develop the skills and mindset needed to make good choices that lead to positive outcomes.

In conclusion, the power of choice is a fundamental concept that we must all understand. The choices we make can have a significant impact on our lives, and it is important to make good choices that align with our values, goals, and aspirations. As teenagers, parents, and individuals seeking personal development, leadership coaching, or life coaching, we must use the power of choice wisely to achieve our full potential and lead fulfilling lives.

The effects of making good and bad choices

The choices we make every day have a significant impact on our lives. Whether we make good or bad decisions, they will shape our future and determine the kind of person we become. In this subchapter, we will discuss the effects of making good and bad choices.

Making good choices can lead to a successful and fulfilling life. When we make good choices, we feel confident, happy, and proud of ourselves. These choices can lead to positive outcomes such as good grades, healthy relationships, and a successful career. Making good choices also helps us develop self-discipline, responsibility, and good habits that will benefit us for a lifetime.

On the other hand, making bad choices can have a negative impact on our lives. Bad choices can lead to poor outcomes such as failing grades, damaged relationships, and even legal trouble. Making bad choices also affects our self-esteem, making us feel guilty, ashamed, and regretful. Bad choices can lead to negative habits such as substance abuse, addiction, and other destructive behaviors that can have long-lasting effects on our mental and physical health.

It is essential for teenagers to understand the consequences of their choices. Parents, life coaching, personal development coaching, and leadership coaching can help teenagers make better choices by guiding them on how to make informed decisions, taking responsibility for their actions, and setting goals for their future. Parents can also provide a supportive and nurturing environment where teenagers can feel safe to express themselves and seek guidance without fear of judgment or punishment.

In conclusion, making good choices can lead to a successful and fulfilling life, while making bad choices can have negative long-term effects on our lives. As teenagers, we should strive to make informed decisions, take responsibility for our actions, and set goals for our future. With the guidance of parents and coaches, we can develop the skills and habits necessary to make good choices and lead a happy and fulfilling life.

MAKING GOOD DECISIONS

Identifying and analyzing options

Identifying and Analyzing Options

As a teenager, you will face many options and choices that will shape your future. These choices can be overwhelming, and it's crucial to learn how to identify and analyze them. The ability to make sound decisions is a crucial skill that will help you navigate through life's challenges and opportunities.

Identifying Options

The first step in making good choices is to identify your options. This means taking the time to explore all the possible choices available to you. Ask yourself questions like "What are my goals?" "What are the possible outcomes?" "What are the pros and cons?" "Who can I seek advice from?" This will help you identify all the possible options and choose the one that aligns with your goals and values.

Analyzing Options

Once you have identified your options, the next step is to analyze them. This means weighing out the pros and cons of each option. Make a list of the advantages and disadvantages of each choice. Next, evaluate how each option aligns with your goals, values, and priorities. Consider the possible outcomes and consequences of each choice. Identify the possible risks and opportunities associated with each option.

Seeking Advice

In some cases, it may be challenging to identify and analyze options. In such situations, seeking advice from trusted individuals like parents, teachers, coaches, or mentors can be helpful. These individuals have more experience and can offer valuable insights and perspectives that can help you make better decisions.

Trusting Your Instincts

In some cases, your instincts may guide you towards the best option. Trusting your instincts can be valuable, especially when you have limited time to make a decision. However, it's important to remember that instincts can be influenced by emotions and biases. Therefore, it's essential to identify and analyze your options before making a decision.

Conclusion

Identifying and analyzing options is a crucial skill that will help you make good choices. It's important to take the time to explore all the possible options, weigh out the pros and cons, seek advice if necessary, and trust your instincts. By doing so, you'll be able to make informed decisions that align with your goals, values, and priorities. Remember, every decision you make shapes your future, so choose wisely.

The importance of setting goals

The importance of setting goals

Goal setting is an important aspect of life that many people overlook. This is especially true for teenagers who are still trying to figure out their way in life. Setting goals can help teenagers focus their energies and achieve their dreams. It can also help them develop a sense of purpose and direction.

One of the key benefits of setting goals is that it helps teenagers develop a sense of motivation. When they have a clear idea of what they want to achieve, they are more likely to work hard and stay focused. This can be especially important for teenagers who are struggling with motivation or who are easily distracted.

Setting goals can also help teenagers develop a sense of responsibility. When they set goals, they are taking ownership of their future and committing to achieving something important. This can help them develop a sense of self-discipline and the ability to follow through on their commitments.

Another benefit of setting goals is that it can help teenagers develop a sense of resilience. When they encounter obstacles or setbacks, having a clear goal in mind can help them stay focused and motivated. They can use their goal as a source of inspiration and motivation to keep going.

Parents can play an important role in helping their teenagers set goals. They can encourage their children to think about their future and what they want to achieve. They can also help them break down their goals into smaller, more manageable steps, and provide support and encouragement along the way.

For life coaching, personal development coaching, and leadership coaching, goal setting is a foundational skill. Coaches can help teenagers develop a clear vision of their future and set goals that align with that vision. They can also provide support and guidance as teenagers work towards achieving their goals.

In conclusion, setting goals is an important skill for teenagers to develop. It can help them focus their energies, develop a sense of purpose and direction, and achieve their dreams. Parents and coaches can play an important role in helping teenagers set goals and providing support and encouragement along the way.

Overcoming fear and taking risks

Overcoming fear and taking risks

Fear is a natural response to unfamiliar situations or potential danger. It can help keep us safe, but it can also hold us back from achieving our goals and living life to the fullest. Taking risks is an essential part of personal growth

Making Good Decisions

and development, but it requires courage and the willingness to step outside of our comfort zones.

The first step in overcoming fear is to acknowledge it. Recognize when fear is holding you back and identify the source of that fear. Often, our fears are based on past experiences or negative self-talk, and it's important to challenge those beliefs and replace them with positive affirmations.

One way to build confidence and overcome fear is through exposure therapy. This involves gradually exposing yourself to the thing that scares you, starting with small steps and increasing the difficulty over time. For example, if you're afraid of public speaking, you could start by speaking in front of a small group of friends and family before working up to larger crowds.

Another strategy for overcoming fear is to reframe your mindset. Instead of seeing failure as a negative outcome, view it as an opportunity to learn and grow. Failure is not the end of the road but a stepping stone to success.

Taking risks can be intimidating, but it's necessary for personal growth and success. Start by setting clear goals and creating a plan of action. Break down your goals into manageable steps and focus on the process rather than the outcome.

It's also important to surround yourself with supportive people who believe in you and your goals. Seek out mentors or join a community of like-minded individuals who can offer guidance and encouragement.

Remember, taking risks doesn't guarantee success, but it does guarantee growth and learning. Don't let fear hold you back from pursuing your dreams and living the life you want. Embrace the unknown, take calculated risks, and trust in your ability to handle whatever comes your way.

Learning from mistakes

Learning from mistakes is a crucial aspect of personal growth and development. It is a fundamental life skill that everyone should learn and master. Making mistakes is inevitable, but how you respond to them is what matters most. As a teen, you are bound to make mistakes, and it is essential to learn from them to avoid repeating them in the future.

Mistakes are not failures but learning opportunities. They offer a chance to reflect on what went wrong and how to do things differently. Therefore, instead of dwelling on the mistake, it is essential to focus on the lesson learned. In this way, you can avoid repeating the same mistake and can make better decisions in the future.

Parents and coaches can assist teens in learning from their mistakes by offering constructive criticism and guidance. They can help them see their mistakes as learning opportunities rather than failures. By doing so, teens can develop a growth mindset that allows them to embrace challenges and learn from them.

Additionally, learning from mistakes requires taking responsibility for your actions. It means acknowledging your mistakes and making amends if necessary. It also means taking steps to correct the mistake and prevent it from happening again. This process requires self-reflection and a willingness to learn and grow.

Moreover, learning from mistakes involves developing resilience. It is essential to bounce back from failure and continue to pursue your goals. Resilience helps teens to cope with setbacks and challenges and to keep moving forward.

In conclusion, learning from mistakes is an essential life skill that everyone should learn. It involves taking responsibility, being resilient, and embracing challenges. As a teen, it is crucial to learn from your mistakes, and parents and coaches can help you develop this skill. Remember that making mistakes is not failure but an opportunity to learn and grow.

DEVELOPING A DECISION-MAKING PROCESS

Understanding the decision-making process

Understanding the Decision-Making Process

Every day, we are faced with decisions that affect our lives, whether it's choosing what to eat for breakfast or deciding on a career path. Making good decisions is an essential part of life, and it's crucial to understand the decision-making process to make informed and wise choices.

The decision-making process is a step-by-step approach that helps us identify and evaluate alternatives to choose the best course of action. It involves six stages: identifying the problem, gathering information, identifying alternatives, evaluating alternatives, choosing the best alternative, and implementing the decision.

Identifying the problem is the first step in the decision-making process. It involves identifying the issue or situation that needs attention, such as a difficult decision or a challenge you're facing. This step requires you to define the problem clearly and determine what needs to be addressed.

The second step is gathering information. This involves researching and gathering data to help you make an informed decision. It's essential to gather as much information as possible to make an informed choice.

The third step is identifying alternatives. This step involves brainstorming different options and alternatives to solve the problem. It's important to consider all possible alternatives, including those that may seem unlikely or unconventional.

The fourth step is evaluating alternatives. This step involves weighing the pros and cons of each alternative and determining which one is the best fit for the situation. It's essential to consider the potential consequences of each alternative.

The fifth step is choosing the best alternative. This step involves selecting the alternative that best addresses the problem and aligns with your values and goals. It's essential to make a decision that feels right and aligns with your values.

The final step is implementing the decision. This step involves putting the decision into action and monitoring the results. It's important to evaluate the outcomes of the decision and make adjustments if necessary.

Understanding the decision-making process can help you make better decisions and avoid common pitfalls. It's essential to take the time to identify the problem, gather information, identify alternatives, evaluate alternatives, choose the best alternative, and implement the decision. By doing so, you can make informed and wise choices that align with your values and goals.

The importance of gathering information

The importance of gathering information

In today's world, information is everywhere. From social media to news outlets, we are constantly bombarded with information. However, not all information is created equal, and it's important to learn how to gather and interpret information effectively. This is especially important for teenagers who are faced with many decisions that can impact their future.

Gathering information is the first step in making informed decisions. It allows you to understand the options available and the possible consequences of each choice. Without gathering information, decisions are made blindly, and the outcome may not be what you had hoped for. Gathering information helps to reduce the risk of making a bad decision.

It is essential to gather information from credible sources. This means seeking information from experts, reliable news sources, and trustworthy websites. In the age of the internet, it's easy to fall prey to fake news and misinformation. Taking the time to verify information is critical in making informed decisions.

Parents can also play a crucial role in helping teenagers gather information. Encouraging open communication and providing access to resources can help teenagers make informed decisions. Parents can also help teenagers identify reliable sources of information and teach them how to evaluate the credibility of sources.

Life coaching, personal development coaching, and leadership coaching can also help teenagers gather information. These coaches can help teenagers identify their goals and provide guidance on how to gather the information necessary to achieve those goals. They can also help teenagers develop critical thinking skills, which are essential for making informed decisions.

In conclusion, gathering information is a crucial step in making informed decisions. With so much information available, it's important to learn how to gather and interpret information effectively. Parents and coaches can play a crucial role in helping teenagers develop this skill. By gathering information from credible sources, teenagers can reduce the risk of making a bad decision and set themselves up for success in the future.

Critical thinking skills

Critical thinking skills are essential for making good decisions in life. As a teen, you are faced with numerous choices that will have long-lasting effects on your life. Critical thinking skills involve analyzing information, evaluating arguments, and making rational and informed decisions. These skills are not only valuable for your personal growth but also for your success in academics, career, and relationships.

The first step in developing critical thinking skills is to question assumptions. You should not accept everything at face value. Instead, you should ask questions to gain a deeper understanding of the situation. You can start by asking questions such as why, how, and what if. This will help you to consider different perspectives and identify any biases or assumptions that may be present.

Another important skill is to evaluate arguments. When presented with an argument, you should analyze the evidence and reasoning behind it. You should consider the source of the information and the credibility of the person presenting the argument. You should also identify any logical fallacies or errors in reasoning.

In addition, critical thinking skills involve making rational and informed decisions. You should weigh the pros and cons of each option and consider the potential consequences. You should also consider your values and beliefs and how they may impact your decision. It is important to make decisions based on facts and evidence rather than emotions or peer pressure.

As a parent, life coach, personal development coach, or leadership coach, it is important to encourage and support the development of critical thinking skills in teens. You can do this by providing opportunities for them to practice these skills, such as engaging in debates or discussions, encouraging them to ask questions, and providing them with information from diverse sources.

In conclusion, critical thinking skills are essential for making good decisions in life. As a teen, it is important to question assumptions, evaluate arguments, and make rational and informed decisions. As a parent or coach, you can support the development of these skills by providing opportunities for practice and encouraging questioning and diverse perspectives.

Identifying and overcoming biases

Identifying and Overcoming Biases

As humans, we all have biases. Biases are our preconceived notions, beliefs, or attitudes towards a person, group, or thing. They can be based on our personal experiences, cultural upbringing, or societal conditioning. However, biases can cloud our judgment and prevent us from making rational decisions. Therefore, it is essential to identify and overcome biases to make good decisions.

Identifying Biases

The first step in overcoming biases is to identify them. We can do this by recognizing our thoughts, emotions, and behavior towards a particular situation or person. For instance, we may have a bias towards a certain race, gender, or religion. We may also have a bias towards people with disabilities, different sexual orientations, or political affiliations.

To identify our biases, we need to ask ourselves some questions. What are my assumptions about this situation or person? Why do I feel this way? Am I being fair and objective? Am I judging based on facts or stereotypes?

Overcoming Biases

Once we have identified our biases, we need to overcome them. Overcoming biases requires an open mind, willingness to learn, and empathy towards others. Here are some ways we can overcome biases:

1. Educate ourselves: We can learn more about different cultures, religions, and lifestyles by reading books, watching documentaries, or

attending cultural events. By educating ourselves, we can challenge our stereotypes and gain a broader perspective.

2. Practice empathy: We can put ourselves in someone else's shoes and try to understand their perspective. We can also listen to their stories and experiences without judgment.

3. Check our assumptions: We can question our assumptions and ask ourselves if they are based on facts or stereotypes. We can also seek feedback from others to get a different perspective.

4. Be aware of our emotions: We can be aware of our emotions and how they influence our judgment. We can take a few deep breaths, pause, and reflect before making a decision.

5. Surround ourselves with diversity: We can surround ourselves with people from different backgrounds, cultures, and lifestyles. By doing so, we can learn from their experiences and perspectives.

Conclusion

Identifying and overcoming biases is an essential skill for making good decisions. By recognizing our biases and taking steps to overcome them, we can become more empathetic, open-minded, and fair in our decision-making. This skill is particularly important for teens who are still developing their worldview and identity. Parents and coaches can also play a vital role in helping teens identify and overcome biases by providing a safe and supportive environment for learning and growth.

CONSEQUENCES OF CHOICES

The ripple effect of choices

The Ripple Effect of Choices

Every choice we make has a ripple effect that can impact our lives and the lives of others. The choices we make today can have consequences that last for years, and it's important to be mindful of the impact our decisions can have.

For teens, this can be especially important to understand. As you navigate the teenage years, you'll be faced with a lot of choices that can shape your future. Whether it's choosing to study for an exam or skipping class, the choices you make can have a significant impact on your academic success and your future opportunities.

But it's not just academic choices that matter. The decisions you make about your relationships, your health, and your personal values can also have a ripple effect on your life. For example, if you choose to engage in risky behaviors like drug use or unprotected sex, you could be putting yourself at risk for long-term health problems and limiting your opportunities in the future.

The ripple effect of choices can also extend beyond our own lives. The decisions we make can impact our families, friends, and communities. For example, if you choose to engage in illegal activities, you could be putting your family at risk of legal consequences or causing harm to your community.

As parents and coaches, it's important to help teens understand the ripple effect of their choices. By helping them develop a sense of responsibility and mindfulness, we can empower them to make choices that have positive consequences.

One way to do this is by encouraging teens to think about the long-term impact of their decisions. Instead of focusing on short-term benefits, encourage them to consider how their choices will impact their future goals and relationships.

Another way to help teens understand the ripple effect of their choices is by modeling responsible decision-making. As parents and coaches, we can set an example by making thoughtful choices and considering the impact of our decisions on ourselves and others.

Ultimately, the ripple effect of choices is a reminder that we all have the power to shape our lives and the lives of those around us. By making mindful and responsible choices, we can create a positive impact that can last a lifetime.

The impact of choices on relationships and reputation

The choices we make have a significant impact on our relationships and reputation. As a teen, it's vital to understand this concept and make decisions that will lead to positive outcomes in both areas.

Relationships are an essential part of our lives, and they require effort, care, and attention. Our choices can either strengthen or weaken these relationships. For instance, choosing to communicate honestly and openly with our friends and family strengthens our relationships with them. On the other hand, lying, gossiping, or being disrespectful can damage our relationships irreparably.

It's essential to understand that every choice we make has consequences. Even seemingly small decisions can have significant effects on our relationships. For example, choosing to ignore a friend's message or canceling plans last minute can hurt their feelings and damage the trust in the relationship.

Additionally, the choices we make can also affect our reputation. Reputation is the way people perceive us and the judgments they make about our character. Our reputation can impact our opportunities, such as job offers, college admissions, and social connections.

The choices we make can either enhance or tarnish our reputation. For instance, choosing to be honest, respectful, and responsible can build a positive reputation. In contrast, making choices that are dishonest, disrespectful, or reckless can damage our reputation and make it difficult to regain trust.

In conclusion, every choice we make has an impact on our relationships and reputation. As teens, it's crucial to make choices that will lead to positive outcomes in both areas. We should strive to be honest, respectful, and responsible in our decisions, which will ultimately lead to healthy relationships and a positive reputation. As parents, Life Coaching , Personal Development Coaching , and Leadership Coaching niches, we should guide our teens towards making good choices and help them understand the consequences of their actions. By doing so, we can empower them to make informed decisions that will shape their lives positively.

The importance of responsibility and accountability

The importance of responsibility and accountability cannot be overstated. As a teenager, you are at a crossroads where every decision you make can have a significant impact on your future. It is essential to understand that every choice you make has consequences, and you are responsible for them.

Responsibility means taking ownership of your actions and their consequences. It is about making conscious decisions and being accountable for their outcomes. As a teenager, you are growing up and learning about the world around you. You are also learning how to make choices that will shape your future. Taking responsibility for your decisions means that you are willing to face the consequences of your actions, whether they are positive or negative.

Accountability goes hand in hand with responsibility. It means being answerable for your actions and their outcomes. When you are accountable, you are willing to accept the consequences of your choices and take steps to rectify any mistakes you may have made. Being accountable also means that you are willing to learn from your mistakes and make better choices in the future.

As a teenager, it is easy to blame others for your mistakes or to make excuses for your behavior. However, this kind of behavior will only lead to more problems in the future. It is crucial to take responsibility for your actions and be accountable for their outcomes. This will help you build trust with others and earn their respect.

Parents and coaches play a significant role in teaching teenagers about responsibility and accountability. They can help teenagers understand the consequences of their choices and encourage them to take ownership of their actions. By providing guidance and support, parents and coaches can help teenagers develop a sense of responsibility and accountability that will serve them well throughout their lives.

In conclusion, responsibility and accountability are essential qualities that every teenager should possess. By taking ownership of your actions and being accountable for their outcomes, you can build trust and earn respect from others. Parents and coaches can help teenagers develop these qualities by providing guidance and support. Remember, every choice you make has consequences, and you are responsible for them. Choose wisely, take ownership of your actions, and be accountable for their outcomes.

OVERCOMING OBSTACLES

Identifying and overcoming obstacles that hinder good decision-making

Identifying and overcoming obstacles that hinder good decision-making

Making good decisions is not always easy, and there are times when we make bad decisions that we regret. However, it is essential to learn from our mistakes and identify the obstacles that hinder good decision-making, so we can overcome them and make better choices in the future.

One of the main obstacles to good decision-making is fear. Fear can prevent us from taking risks, and it can also make us hesitant and indecisive. To overcome fear, we need to face it head-on and take small steps towards our goals. It is also important to have a support system in place, whether it is family, friends, or a mentor, who can encourage us and provide guidance when we need it.

Another obstacle to good decision-making is lack of knowledge or information. When we do not have all the facts, we may make decisions based on assumptions or incomplete information, which can lead to poor outcomes. To overcome this, we need to do our research, ask questions, and seek advice from experts or those with more experience.

Distractions can also hinder good decision-making, whether it is social media, peer pressure, or other distractions that take us away from our goals. To overcome distractions, we need to prioritize our time and focus on what is important. We can also set goals and create a plan of action to help us stay on track.

Finally, negative self-talk can also hinder good decision-making. When we doubt ourselves or have negative beliefs about our abilities, we may make decisions based on fear or insecurity. To overcome negative self-talk, we need to challenge our beliefs and focus on our strengths and accomplishments. We can also practice positive self-talk and affirmations to build our confidence and make better decisions.

In conclusion, identifying and overcoming obstacles that hinder good decision-making is essential for personal growth and success. By facing our fears, gathering information, staying focused, and believing in ourselves, we can make better choices and achieve our goals.

Peer pressure and its impact on decision-making

Peer pressure is one of the most pervasive social influences that impact our decision-making, especially during our teenage years. It is the pressure we feel from our peers to conform to their expectations, behaviors, and attitudes. Peer pressure can be both positive and negative, but it often leads us to make choices that are not in our best interest.

As a teen, you may feel the need to fit in, to be liked, and to be accepted by your peers. This can lead you to make decisions that are not aligned with your values, goals, or interests. You may be tempted to engage in risky behaviors like drinking, smoking, or drug use because your friends are doing it. You may also feel pressured to conform to certain social norms like dressing a certain way, listening to certain music, or participating in certain activities.

The impact of peer pressure on decision-making can be significant. When you feel pressure from your peers, you may experience anxiety, stress, and fear of rejection. These emotions can cloud your judgment and impair your ability to make good decisions. You may also feel a sense of guilt or shame if you go against the wishes of your friends.

Parents and coaches can play a critical role in helping teens navigate peer pressure and make good decisions. They can encourage teens to develop a strong sense of self-awareness, self-esteem, and self-confidence. They can also teach teens to identify their values, goals, and interests and make decisions that align with them.

Additionally, parents and coaches can help teens build healthy relationships with their peers. They can encourage teens to surround themselves with positive influences and avoid negative influences. They can also teach teens to communicate effectively with their peers and assert their boundaries when necessary.

In conclusion, peer pressure is a powerful force that can impact our decision-making, especially during our teenage years. However, with the right guidance, support, and tools, teens can learn to make good decisions that align with their values, goals, and interests. Parents and coaches can play a critical role in helping teens navigate peer pressure and develop strong decision-making skills.

Managing stress and emotions

Managing stress and emotions is a crucial aspect of making good decisions as a teenager. It is normal to experience stress and a range of emotions, but it is important to develop healthy coping mechanisms to deal with them. Stress and emotions can be overwhelming at times, leading to poor decision-making and negative consequences.

One effective way of managing stress is through mindfulness practices. Mindfulness involves being present in the moment, observing your thoughts and emotions without judgment. It can help you become more aware of your stress triggers and develop strategies to deal with them. Some mindfulness practices include meditation, deep breathing exercises, and yoga.

Another way of managing stress is through physical activity. Exercise can boost your mood, reduce stress, and improve your overall well-being. It is recommended that teenagers get at least 60 minutes of physical activity each day. This can include activities such as walking, biking, or joining a sports team.

In addition to managing stress, it is important to learn how to regulate your emotions. Emotions can be powerful and overwhelming, but it is possible to learn how to manage them effectively. One way of doing this is through emotional regulation techniques such as deep breathing, journaling, or talking to a trusted friend or family member. It is also important to recognize when you need help and seek support from a mental health professional if necessary.

As a teenager, it is normal to experience a range of emotions, including anger, sadness, and anxiety. However, it is important to learn how to express these emotions in a healthy way. This can involve practicing effective communication skills, such as using "I" statements and active listening. It can also involve finding healthy outlets for your emotions, such as art, music, or writing.

In conclusion, managing stress and emotions is a critical aspect of making good decisions as a teenager. By developing healthy coping mechanisms and learning how to regulate your emotions, you can improve your overall well-being and make better decisions. Remember, it is okay to ask for help when you need it, and there are resources available to support you.

BUILDING SELF-CONFIDENCE

The importance of self-confidence in decision-making

The Importance of Self-Confidence in Decision-Making

Making decisions can be a tough process, especially for teenagers who are still trying to figure out who they are and what they want in life. But one of the most important factors that can help a teen make good decisions is self-confidence. In this subchapter, we will explore why self-confidence is crucial for decision-making and how it can be developed.

Self-confidence is the belief in oneself and one's abilities. It is the foundation for success, happiness, and fulfillment in life. A lack of self-confidence can lead to indecisiveness, self-doubt, and anxiety. On the other hand, a high level of self-confidence can give a teen the courage to take risks, make tough decisions, and pursue their dreams.

When it comes to decision-making, self-confidence plays a significant role. A teen who lacks confidence may hesitate to make decisions, second-guess themselves, and ultimately make the wrong choice. Conversely, a teen who is self-assured will trust their gut instinct, weigh the pros and cons, and make a decision with conviction.

So how can a teenager develop self-confidence and become a better decision-maker? The first step is to identify their strengths and weaknesses. By focusing on their strengths, they can build their self-esteem and feel more confident in their abilities. Additionally, they can work on developing their skills and knowledge in areas where they feel less confident.

Another important factor in building self-confidence is surrounding oneself with positive and supportive people. Family, friends, and mentors can provide encouragement, guidance, and validation. A teen should seek out these relationships and nurture them.

Finally, self-care is vital for building self-confidence. Exercise, healthy eating, and practicing mindfulness can all help to reduce stress and increase feelings of self-worth. When a teen feels good about themselves, they are more likely to trust their decision-making abilities.

In conclusion, self-confidence is essential for making good decisions. By building self-confidence through self-awareness, positive relationships, and self-care, a teenager can become a confident and decisive individual, ready to tackle any challenge that comes their way.

Building self-confidence through self-awareness and self-acceptance

Building self-confidence through self-awareness and self-acceptance is crucial for teens to develop a strong sense of self and make good decisions in life. Self-awareness is the ability to recognize and understand your own thoughts, feelings, and behaviors, while self-acceptance is the ability to accept and love yourself for who you are.

As a teen, it is normal to struggle with self-doubt and insecurities, especially in a world where social media and peer pressure can create unrealistic standards of beauty, success, and popularity. However, by developing self-awareness, you can gain a better understanding of your strengths and weaknesses, values and beliefs, and goals and aspirations. This can help you identify your passions, talents, and interests, and build your confidence in pursuing them.

Self-acceptance is also crucial for building self-confidence because it allows you to embrace your unique qualities and accept yourself for who you are, rather than comparing yourself to others or trying to meet others' expectations. Accepting yourself for who you are can be challenging, but it is essential for developing self-esteem and resilience, and for building healthy relationships with others.

Parents can play a crucial role in helping their teens build self-confidence through self-awareness and self-acceptance by creating a supportive and accepting environment where their children can express themselves freely and explore their interests and passions. Parents can also encourage their children to develop a growth mindset and focus on their efforts and progress rather than their achievements and failures.

Life coaching, personal development coaching, and leadership coaching can also help teens build self-confidence by providing them with tools and strategies to develop their self-awareness, self-acceptance, and self-esteem. Coaches can help teens identify their strengths and weaknesses, set goals and priorities, and overcome obstacles and challenges. They can also teach them how to manage their emotions and thoughts, develop healthy habits and routines, and build positive relationships with themselves and others.

In conclusion, building self-confidence through self-awareness and self-acceptance is a lifelong journey, but it is a worthwhile one that can lead to a happier, healthier, and more fulfilling life. By developing self-awareness and self-acceptance, teens can gain a better understanding of themselves, build their confidence, and make good decisions that align with their values and goals. Parents and coaches can play a crucial role in supporting teens on this journey and helping them reach their full potential.

Developing a positive self-image

Developing a Positive Self-Image

One of the most important things you can do for yourself is to develop a positive self-image. This means seeing yourself in a positive light and believing in your abilities and worth as a person. A positive self-image is essential for building self-confidence, making good decisions, and achieving success in life.

Here are some tips for developing a positive self-image:

1. Focus on your strengths: Everyone has strengths and weaknesses. Instead of dwelling on your weaknesses, focus on your strengths. What are you good at? What do people praise you for? Build on these strengths and use them to your advantage.

2. Stop comparing yourself to others: It's easy to fall into the trap of comparing yourself to others, but this only leads to feelings of inadequacy and low self-esteem. Remember that everyone has their own unique talents and abilities, and it's okay to be different.

3. Practice positive self-talk: The way you talk to yourself can have a huge impact on your self-image. Instead of criticizing yourself, practice positive self-talk. Tell yourself that you are capable, smart, and deserving of success.

4. Surround yourself with positive influences: Surrounding yourself with positive people and influences can help boost your self-esteem and self-

image. Seek out friends and mentors who support and encourage you.

5. Take care of yourself: Taking care of your physical and mental health is essential for developing a positive self-image. Eat well, exercise regularly, and get enough sleep. Practice self-care activities like meditation, yoga, or journaling.

Remember, developing a positive self-image takes time and effort. It's important to be patient with yourself and to celebrate your successes along the way. With a positive self-image, you can achieve anything you set your mind to.

COMMUNICATION SKILLS

The role of communication in decision-making

The role of communication in decision-making

Effective communication is the cornerstone of good decision-making. Communication involves sharing information, ideas, and opinions with others, and it is crucial to making informed decisions. As a teenager, you are likely to face many situations where you need to make decisions that will shape your future. Whether it is choosing a career path, deciding where to go to college, or navigating complex social situations, effective communication is essential.

Communication is not just about talking, but also about listening. It is important to listen carefully to what others have to say, especially when you are making decisions that will affect them. Active listening can help you understand the perspectives of others and make better-informed decisions. It is also essential to communicate clearly and concisely to ensure that others understand your point of view.

In decision-making, communication can help you gather information and insights from others. It can also help you build consensus and support for your decisions. When you involve others in the decision-making process, they are more likely to feel invested in the outcome and be more supportive of your decision.

Parents and coaches can play a crucial role in helping teenagers develop their communication skills. They can provide guidance and feedback on how to communicate effectively and encourage them to practice their skills in different situations. Parents can also model effective communication by listening actively and communicating clearly with their children.

In summary, effective communication is essential to making good decisions. It involves sharing information, listening carefully, and building consensus with others. As a teenager, you can develop your communication skills by practicing active listening, communicating clearly, and involving others in your decision-making process. Parents and coaches can play an essential role in helping teenagers develop their communication skills, which will serve them well throughout their lives.

Active listening and effective communication

Active listening and effective communication are essential life skills that can help you in all aspects of your life, from school and work to friendships and family relationships. Active listening means being fully present and focused on what the other person is saying, both verbally and non-verbally. Effective communication means expressing yourself clearly and respectfully, while also being open to hearing other people's perspectives.

One of the key components of active listening is paying attention to non-verbal cues. This includes things like eye contact, body language, and tone of voice. By paying attention to these cues, you can better understand the emotions and intentions behind what someone is saying. Additionally, it's important to avoid interrupting or jumping to conclusions. Instead, give the other person the space and time to fully express themselves before responding.

Effective communication involves both verbal and non-verbal skills. When expressing yourself, it's important to speak clearly and confidently, while also being mindful of your body language and tone of voice. It's also important to use "I" statements instead of "you" statements, which can come across as accusatory or confrontational. For example, instead of saying "You always make me feel like I'm not good enough," try saying "I feel really insecure when I don't get positive feedback."

In addition to expressing yourself clearly, effective communication also involves actively listening to other people's perspectives. This means being open-minded and curious, and trying to understand where the other person is coming from. Even if you don't agree with their perspective, it's important to show respect and empathy for their views.

Overall, active listening and effective communication are vital skills for navigating relationships and making good decisions. By practicing these skills, you can improve your communication with others and build stronger, more meaningful connections in your life.

Assertiveness and setting boundaries

Assertiveness and Setting Boundaries

Assertiveness is an essential skill that everyone needs to master. It is the ability to express your thoughts and feelings in a clear, direct, and respectful way. Being assertive means standing up for yourself while also respecting the rights and feelings of others. It is a key aspect of healthy relationships, effective communication, and personal development.

Setting boundaries is an important part of assertiveness. A boundary is a limit that you set for yourself or others. It defines what is acceptable and what is not. Boundaries help you protect your time, energy, and emotions. They also help you communicate your needs and expectations to others.

As a teen, you may find it challenging to be assertive and set boundaries. You may feel pressure to fit in, please others, or avoid conflict. However, being passive or aggressive can lead to problems in your relationships, self-esteem, and decision-making. Learning to be assertive and set boundaries can help you build self-confidence, improve communication, and make better choices.

Here are some tips for developing assertiveness and setting boundaries:

1. Know your values and priorities. Take time to reflect on what matters most to you in life. Identify your goals, interests, and beliefs. This will help you clarify your needs and assert them with confidence.

2. Practice assertive communication. Use "I" statements to express your thoughts and feelings. For example, instead of saying "You always ignore me," say "I feel upset when you don't listen to me." Use a calm and respectful tone of voice, and avoid blaming or attacking others.

3. Set clear boundaries. Identify what behaviors are acceptable and unacceptable to you. Communicate your boundaries clearly and assertively. For example, "I don't like it when you tease me about my appearance. Please stop."

4. Be consistent. Stick to your boundaries and follow through on your assertive communication. Don't let others manipulate or guilt-trip you into breaking your boundaries. Remember, you have the right to say no and prioritize your own needs.

5. Seek support. If you struggle with assertiveness or setting boundaries, seek guidance from a trusted adult, counselor, or coach. They can help you develop skills and strategies for healthy relationships and personal growth.

In conclusion, assertiveness and setting boundaries are crucial skills for teens and adults alike. By practicing assertive communication and setting clear boundaries, you can build self-confidence, improve relationships, and make better choices. Remember, you have the power of choice to assert your needs and prioritize your well-being.

CONCLUSION

The importance of making good choices for a fulfilling life

The choices we make in life define who we are and shape our future. They determine the path we take and the kind of person we become. Making good choices is essential for a fulfilling life, and it is something that every teen should learn.

The teenage years are a defining period in a person's life. It is a time when you are discovering who you are and what you want to do with your life. It is also a time when you are faced with many choices, some of which can have a significant impact on your future. This is why it is important to learn how to make good choices.

Good choices are those that align with your values, beliefs, and goals. They are choices that lead to positive outcomes and help you grow as a person. Making good choices requires self-awareness, critical thinking, and the ability to consider the consequences of your actions.

One of the biggest challenges teens face is peer pressure. It can be tempting to follow the crowd, even if it means making bad choices. However, it is important to remember that you are in control of your life, and you have the power to make your own choices. It is okay to say no to things that do not align with your values or goals.

Parents and coaches play a vital role in helping teens make good choices. They can provide guidance, support, and encouragement, as well as help teens develop the skills they need to make good decisions. Parents should create an open and honest dialogue with their teens, where they can discuss their concerns and offer advice. Coaches can provide tools and strategies that help teens develop critical thinking and decision-making skills.

In conclusion, making good choices is essential for a fulfilling life. It requires self-awareness, critical thinking, and the ability to consider the consequences of your actions. Parents and coaches can play a crucial role in helping teens make good choices and develop the skills they need to succeed in life. With the right guidance and support, every teen can learn to make good choices and create a bright future for themselves.

The power of choice and its impact on one's future

The power of choice and its impact on one's future is a topic that cannot be overemphasized. It is a fundamental principle that every teenager must understand and imbibe in order to make good decisions that will shape their future. Choices are a part of life, and every day, we are faced with numerous options that require us to make decisions that will have long-lasting effects on our lives.

The power of choice is the ability to make decisions based on our personal desires, values, and beliefs. It is the freedom to choose our actions and the path we want to take in life. As teenagers, the choices we make can have a significant impact on our future. From the decision to go to college or not, to the choice of friends, and the decision to engage in risky behaviors, every choice we make can either positively or negatively affect our future.

Parents and coaches play a crucial role in helping teenagers understand the power of choice and its impact on their future. They can guide teenagers to make good decisions by teaching them how to weigh the consequences of their actions and make informed choices. Parents and coaches can also teach teenagers how to set goals and identify the steps they need to take to achieve them. By doing so, teenagers will be able to make choices that align with their goals and aspirations.

The power of choice is a tool that can be used to build a successful future. It is the foundation upon which personal development, leadership, and life coaching are built. By teaching teenagers how to make good choices, parents and coaches are equipping them with the skills they need to succeed in life.

In conclusion, the power of choice cannot be overstated. It is a fundamental principle that every teenager must understand and apply in their daily lives. Parents and coaches play a crucial role in helping teenagers navigate the choices they face and make decisions that will positively impact their future. With the right guidance and support, teenagers can harness the power of choice to create a bright and successful future for themselves.

Final thoughts and encouragement for readers

Final Thoughts and Encouragement for Readers

Congratulations on making it this far in your journey towards making good decisions! You have already taken the first step towards achieving your goals and becoming the best version of yourself. As you near the end of this book, we want to leave you with some final thoughts and encouragement to help you continue on your path of personal growth.

Firstly, remember that making good decisions is a lifelong process. It is not something that you can achieve overnight or through a single book. It takes practice, patience, and perseverance. It is important to stay committed to the process and to continue learning and growing every day.

Secondly, it is important to surround yourself with positive influences. Your environment can greatly impact your decision-making abilities. Seek out friends and mentors who share your values and who will encourage you to make good choices. Avoid negative influences that may lead you down the wrong path.

Thirdly, always remember that you have the power of choice. You have the power to choose your thoughts, your actions, and your reactions. No matter what life throws at you, you always have the power to choose how you respond. This is a powerful tool that can help you overcome any obstacle and achieve any goal.

Lastly, we want to encourage you to never give up on yourself. You are capable of achieving great things and making a positive impact on the world around you. If you ever feel discouraged or uncertain, remember that you are not alone. Seek out support from family, friends, or a coach who can help you stay on track.

In conclusion, we hope this book has provided you with valuable insights and tools to help you make good decisions. Remember, the power of choice is in your hands. Use it wisely and continue to strive towards your goals. We believe in you!

RESOURCES

Additional reading materials and resources for teens and parents

In today's world, there is no shortage of reading materials and resources available for teens and parents alike. Whether you're looking for guidance on personal development, leadership skills, or simply seeking advice on how to navigate life's challenges, there are countless books, websites, and other resources available to help you along the way.

Here are some of our top picks for additional reading materials and resources that we believe can be particularly helpful for teens and parents:

1. "The 7 Habits of Highly Effective Teens" by Sean Covey – This best-selling book offers practical

advice and tools for teens looking to build leadership skills, set goals, and make good decisions.

2. "The Whole-Brain Child" by Daniel J. Siegel and Tina Payne Bryson – This book offers insights into how the brain works and provides practical strategies for parents to help their children develop emotional intelligence, resilience, and other key life skills.

3. "Mindset: The New Psychology of Success" by Carol S. Dweck – This book explores the power of mindset and how adopting a growth mindset can help teens and parents achieve greater success in all areas of life.

4. "The 5 Love Languages of Teenagers" by Gary Chapman – This book offers insights into how to communicate effectively with teenagers and build strong, healthy relationships with them.

5. "The Confidence Code for Girls" by Katty Kay and Claire Shipman – This book offers practical advice and insights on how to build confidence and self-esteem in young girls.

In addition to these books, there are also a number of websites and online resources that can be helpful for teens and parents looking for additional guidance and support. Some of our top picks include:

1. TeenLife – This website offers a wealth of resources for teens and parents, including information on summer programs, gap year opportunities, and other educational resources.

2. The Gottman Institute – This website offers resources and tools for parents looking to build stronger, more positive relationships with their children.

3. ReachOut – This website is focused on providing mental health resources and support for young people, including information on depression, anxiety, and other mental health issues.

4. The National Parenting Center – This website offers articles, resources, and product reviews for parents looking to navigate the challenges of raising children in today's world.

Overall, there is no shortage of resources available to help teens and parents navigate the challenges of life and build the skills and knowledge they need to succeed. By taking advantage of these resources and continuing to learn and grow, both teens and parents can build a brighter future for themselves and those around them.

Tools and exercises for developing decision-making skills

Tools and exercises for developing decision-making skills

Making good decisions is a critical skill that can make or break a person's life. It is a skill that requires practice, and the right tools and exercises can help develop this skill. In this chapter, we will discuss some of the practical tools and exercises that can help teens, parents, and coaches develop strong decision-making skills.

1. Mind Mapping

Mind mapping is a powerful tool for visualizing ideas and organizing thoughts. It is a technique that can help you to break down complex problems and make better decisions. Using a mind map, you can identify the pros and cons of a decision, potential outcomes, and risks. It is a great tool for brainstorming and problem-solving.

2. Pros and Cons List

One of the simplest tools for decision-making is the pros and cons list. It is a list of the advantages and disadvantages of a particular decision. It helps to weigh the pros and cons and make an informed decision. This technique is effective for quick decisions that do not require much analysis.

3. Role-playing

Role-playing is a technique that allows you to practice decision-making in a safe and controlled environment. It is a great tool for developing communication skills, empathy, and critical thinking. You can simulate different scenarios and practice making decisions based on the information available.

4. Visualization

Visualization is a powerful tool for developing decision-making skills. It involves imagining the outcome of a decision and how it would affect your life. By visualizing the outcome, you can better understand the consequences of your decision and make an informed choice.

5. Reflection

Reflection is a critical tool for developing decision-making skills. It involves analyzing past decisions and their outcomes. By reflecting on past decisions, you can identify patterns and learn from mistakes. Reflection helps to develop self-awareness and critical thinking skills.

In conclusion, decision-making is a critical skill that can make a significant impact on one's life. The tools and exercises discussed in this chapter can help to develop strong decision-making skills. By practicing and using these tools, teens, parents, and coaches can make informed decisions and lead fulfilling lives.

List of recommended life coaching, personal development coaching, and leadership coaching resources.

List of recommended life coaching, personal development coaching, and leadership coaching resources

If you're looking to improve your life and develop your leadership skills, there's no shortage of resources available to you. Here are some of our top recommendations for books, courses, and coaches to help you on your journey.

Books:

1. The 7 Habits of Highly Effective Teens by Sean Covey - This classic book is a must-read for any teen looking to improve their personal and leadership skills.

2. Mindset: The New Psychology of Success by Carol Dweck - This book explores the power of a growth mindset and how it can help you achieve your goals.

3. The Power of Positive Thinking by Norman Vincent Peale - This book is a timeless classic that teaches you how to think positively and overcome obstacles in life.

4. The Art of Possibility by Rosamund Stone Zander and Benjamin Zander - This book offers a unique perspective on leadership and personal development, encouraging readers to approach life with an open mind and a sense of possibility.

Courses:

1. Yale's Happiness Course - This free online course teaches the science of happiness and provides practical strategies for improving your mood and overall well-being.

2. Mindfulness-Based Stress Reduction (MBSR) - This eight-week course teaches mindfulness meditation techniques that can help you reduce stress and improve your mental health.

3. The Leadership Challenge - This course is designed to help you develop your leadership skills and become a more effective leader in your personal and professional life.

Coaches:

1. Tony Robbins - Tony Robbins is a well-known life coach who has helped millions of people achieve success and happiness in their lives.

2. Marie Forleo - Marie Forleo is a business and life coach who helps people build successful businesses and live their best lives.

3. Brendon Burchard - Brendon Burchard is a high-performance coach who helps people achieve their goals and live a more fulfilling life.

No matter where you are on your personal or leadership journey, there are resources available to help you achieve your goals. Whether you choose to read books, take courses, or work with a coach, the most important thing is to take action and keep moving forward. With the right mindset and tools, you can create the life you want and become the leader you were meant to be.

www.ingramcontent.com/pod-product-compliance
Lightning Source LLC
La Vergne TN
LVHW051427080426
835508LV00022B/3277